ELIZABETH I

& THE ARMADA

BY

JOHN GUY

THE YOUNG ELIZABETH

*T*hroughout her life Elizabeth put great store by being 'mere English', unlike her half-sister, Mary, whose mother, Catherine of Aragon, was Spanish. It was probably why she was so popular with her people, giving them a sense of national pride in a world dominated by Spain. Elizabeth never left English shores, not even to visit Wales, ancestral home of the Tudor dynasty.

RECONCILED

When Henry VIII died in 1547 Elizabeth was just 13 years old. The king had mostly ignored her but, thanks to the efforts of Catherine Parr, Henry's last wife, she was reconciled with her father in the last few years of his life.

IMPRISONED IN THE TOWER

In 1554 Elizabeth was imprisoned in the Tower of London because of her suspected involvement in Sir Thomas Wyatt's rebellion against Mary I's marriage to Philip of Spain.

The dates given in this book are in accordance with the Julian calendar, still being used at the time in Englan

TRAGIC MOTHER

When Henry VIII's first wife, Catherine of Aragon, proved unable to bear him a son, the king took many mistresses, among whom was Anne Boleyn. They married, in secret, in January 1533, when Anne was already with child. Henry was gravely disappointed that Elizabeth was not the son he so desperately wanted as an heir and had little more to do with the young princess. He also soon tired of Anne and accused her of adultery, a 'crime' for which she was later executed in 1536.

VIRTUAL PRISONER

Elizabeth was an elegant, rather than a beautiful woman, of slim build with a fiery shock of red hair. She spent much of her early life a virtual prisoner, confined to several royal palaces, which probably accounts for her studious nature.

EVENTS OF ELIZABETH'S LIFE

~1491~
Henry VIII born
(Elizabeth's father)

~1502~
Anne Boleyn born
(Elizabeth's mother)

~1516~
Princess Mary born
(later Mary I)

~1533~
Henry VIII & Anne Boleyn marry.
Princess Elizabeth born
(later Elizabeth I).
Act of Appeals asserts England's independence from Rome

CHILDHOOD HOME

Elizabeth was born at Greenwich Palace on 7th September 1533. She was taken soon after birth to Hatfield House, Hertfordshire, where she spent most of her early life.

AN EXCEPTIONAL PUPIL

Roger Ascham was appointed as Elizabeth's private tutor. She was his brightest pupil and displayed an exceptional flair for languages.

ich was 10 days behind the Gregorian calendar, used by the Spanish since 1582 and now in universal use.

THE PATH TO THE THRONE

A QUEEN FOR NINE DAYS

Edward VI conferred the throne on his cousin, and childhood sweetheart, Lady Jane Grey. She ruled for just nine days before relinquishing the crown to Mary, Edward's half-sister, and was afterwards executed for treason.

*L*ike her father, Henry VIII, Elizabeth was not born to rule and could never have expected to succeed to the throne. She was third in line after her half-brother Edward and half-sister Mary. Henry had several illegitimate children, including a son, Henry Fitzroy, by his mistress Elizabeth Blount in 1519. The king created him Duke of Richmond in 1525 and began grooming him for the throne. It was only after his untimely death in 1536 that Elizabeth was even considered a possible heir.

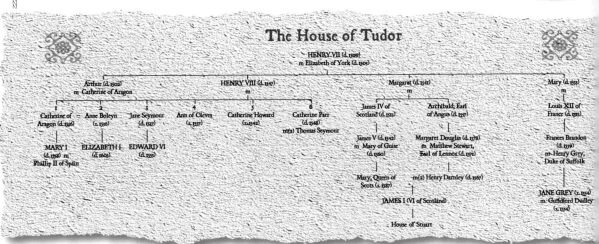

The House of Tudor

HENRY VII (d. 1509)
m Elizabeth of York (d. 1503)

Arthur (d. 1502)
m Catherine of Aragon

HENRY VIII (d. 1547)
m

Margaret (d. 1541)
m

Mary (d. 1533)
m

1 Catherine of Aragon (d. 1536)
2 Anne Boleyn (c. 1536)
3 Jane Seymour (d. 1537)
4 Ann of Cleves (d. 1557)
5 Catherine Howard (c. 1542)
6 Catherine Parr (d. 1548) m(2) Thomas Seymour

James IV of Scotland (d. 1513)

Archibald, Earl of Angus (d. 1557)

Louis XII of France (d. 1515)

MARY I (d. 1558) m Phillip II of Spain

ELIZABETH I (d. 1603)

EDWARD VI (d. 1553)

James V (d. 1542) m Mary of Guise (d. 1560)

Margaret Douglas (d. 1578) m Matthew Stewart, Earl of Lennox (d. 1571)

Frances Brandon (d. 1559) m Henry Grey, Duke of Suffolk

Mary, Queen of Scots (c. 1587)

m(2) Henry Darnley (d. 1567)

JANE GREY (c. 1554) m Guildford Dudley (c. 1554)

JAMES I (VI of Scotland)

House of Stuart

FAMILY TREE

Family Tree showing Elizabeth's path to the throne and her relationship to Edward and Mary. All three of Henry's surviving children were born to different wives.

BOY KING

Edward VI succeeded to the throne in 1547, aged just nine, as Henry's only surviving legitimate male heir.

THE *LIBER REGALIS* OR CORONATION BOOK

Made in 1382 this book is believed to have been used at every coronation from Henry IV to Elizabeth I. Like many others of the time, Elizabeth put great store in astrology and ordered the astrologer John Dee to choose the most advantageous day for her coronation service. So it was that, although she ascended the throne on 17th November 1558, Elizabeth was not crowned until 15th January 1559.

THE KING'S DYING WISH

This anti-papal painting of Henry VIII's deathbed shows the king pointing to Edward as his successor. According to Henry's last will, dated 30th December 1546, succession was to pass first to Mary, then Elizabeth, should anything happen to his son.

FAMILY MATTERS

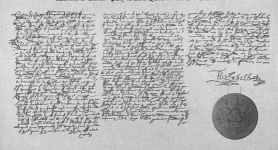

Warrant to Execute Mary Stuart, Queen of Scots. A.D. 1587.

A TRAGIC END

Aware that Mary had herself been used as a pawn in the political struggle for power, Elizabeth was reluctant to sign her death warrant. After 19 years of imprisonment, she was finally executed in 1587.

*E*lizabeth succeeded to the throne at 25 years of age amidst political and religious upheaval. Not least of her problems were the intrigues going on within her own family in an attempt to place a Catholic back on the throne of England. Her cousin Mary, Queen of Scotland in her own right and Elizabeth's closest relative, became embroiled in a plot (almost certainly against her will) to place her on the English throne. Elizabeth, for her part, tried to ensure the line of succession remained in Protestant hands by persuading Mary to marry one of her own favourites.

MARY TAKES FLIGHT

David Rizzio was murdered in front of Mary, Queen of Scots, in 1566. He was Mary's private secretary and was suspected of being her lover. Her husband, Robert Darnley, was implicated in the plot and a year later he himself was murdered. The following year, suspected of involvement in Darnley's death, she fled to England in exile.

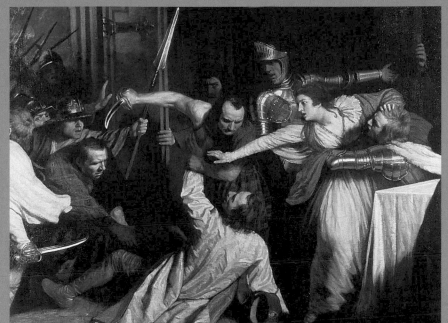

SECRET LIAISONS

There were many suitors for Elizabeth's hand in marriage, the most notable being Robert Dudley, who lived at Kenilworth Castle. But he was already married to Amy Robsart. Amy tragically broke her neck amidst mysterious circumstances, implicating both Elizabeth and Dudley. To avoid further suspicion, perhaps, they did not marry. Instead, Elizabeth tried, unsuccessfully, to marry him off to her Catholic cousin, Mary, Queen of Scots. Instead, Mary married Lord Darnley, a Catholic.

These two views of Kenilworth Castle, in Warwickshire, show: the castle as it appears today in ruins and, below, as it would have looked at the time of Elizabeth's visit in 1575.

THE ROYAL 'PROGRESSES'

Elizabeth frequently took her court on tours, or 'progresses', around the country. Courtiers considered it an honour to be included on the royal tour, even though the cost might bankrupt them. Her longest visit was with Robert Dudley, at Kenilworth, in 1575, when she stayed for 19 days, feasting, hunting and enjoying lavish entertainment.

ELIZABETHAN COURT

The Elizabethan court was more than just an occasion for socialising, though undoubtedly entertainment formed a very important part of proceedings. All of the important decisions of government were made at court. It was also the place where ambitious politicians jostled for power and sought the queen's favours. To be seen at court was essential for personal advancement. Elizabeth had several favourites during the course of her long reign, the most notable in later years being Robert Devereux, Earl of Essex, whom she seems to have genuinely loved. She is said to have been devastated when he betrayed her and she was forced to sign his execution warrant for treason in 1601.

HAND IN GLOVE

Elizabeth was proud of her beautiful hands and often wore elegant gloves to show them off.

YOUNG LOVE

Robert Devereux, 2nd Earl of Essex, was just 20 years old when the ageing Elizabeth first fell under his charms in 1587. Although 34 years his senior, the queen loved him dearly. She forgave his impetuosity and conferred many honours upon him. Their unlikely romance lasted 12 years.

RIGHT-HAND MAN

Sir William Cecil, Principal Secretary of State, was Elizabeth's right-hand man in all matters of government until his death in 1598. He accompanied her at court and on her many 'progresses'.

THE PRICE OF VANITY

Ladies at court had to wear tight corsets, with metal or wooden stays, beneath their clothes to make them look as slim as possible above the bustle of their long gowns. This unique garment belonged to Elizabeth and was used on her funeral effigy

QUEEN OF THE DANCE

Life at Elizabeth's court was often a lively affair. She is seen here dancing with Robert Dudley, Earl of Leicester, who asked for, but was refused, her hand in marriage.

CHIVALROUS BEHAVIOUR

Sir Walter Raleigh was one of Elizabeth's great favourites. Though it is doubtful if he ever did spread his cloak before her, his behaviour was very chivalrous towards her.

EVENTS OF ELIZABETH'S LIFE

~1549~
Cranmer's English Prayer Book published

~1553~
Edward VI dies.
Mary I crowned.
Sir Hugh Willoughby leads expedition to find N.E. Passage

~1554~
Elizabeth imprisoned in Tower of London.
Mary I marries Philip of Spain.
Thomas Wyatt executed.
Lady Jane Grey executed

~1558~
Mary I dies

THE BEGINNINGS OF AN EMPIRE...

*T*he Elizabethan period really was an age of adventure and discovery when, for the first time, English mariners, such as Drake, Willoughby and Frobisher, sailed beyond their immediate shores and explored the very limits of the known world. New trade routes were opened up between such places as North and South America, Russia, Persia and India. Merchants bought, or exchanged home-produced items for exotic goods, bringing untold wealth to Britain.

GIFT FROM A QUEEN

When Drake returned from his circumnavigation of the world, he gave Elizabeth a coconut as a memento. She had a magnificent silver cup made to encase it, which she afterwards presented to him in thanks.

CULINARY DELIGHTS

Several of the newly introduced herbs and spices were used for culinary purposes to disguise the often rancid taste of Elizabethan food.

FROM THE NEW WORLD

These American Indians, from Virginia, are eating maize, one of the many foods discovered in the 'New World'.

THE SPICE OF LIFE

Some of the spices imported
from the Americas, Asia and
the Middle East also had
medicinal properties,
such as nutmeg – used,
sparingly, for various
digestive disorders.

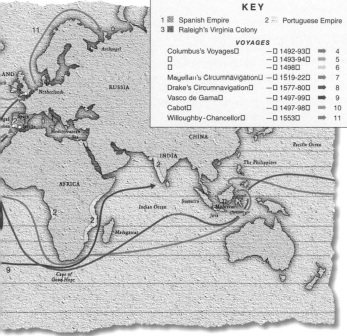

COLONY THAT FAILED

Sir Walter Raleigh established a new
colony in North America in 1584,
which he named Virginia, after
Elizabeth, the 'Virgin Queen', but its
initial success was short-lived and by
1590 it was deserted.

DRESSING FOR DINNER

Chillies, peppers
and other exotic
foods introduced
from the Americas,
were used in cooking
as a flavouring, or
sprinkled on salads
as a condiment.

WORLD EXPLORATION

The map above shows the principal new trade routes
opened up by the Elizabethan explorers, bringing cheap
new goods to Britain from all regions of the world.

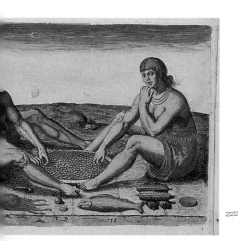

KILL OR CURE

Sir John Hawkins introduced
tobacco to England from
America (where the native
Indians smoked it in clay
pipes) in about 1565.
Originally, it was used as
a medicine to purge the
body of phlegm.

...THE BEGINNINGS OF AN EMPIRE

*T*he King of Spain, Philip II, had hoped to unite the throne of England and Spain by marrying Mary I, but his plans were foiled when she died in 1558. Instead, England became a thorn in his side. What had begun as a small group of privateers stealing Spain's wealth in a series of piratical raids, turned into a more serious quest for power. As England's naval commanders became ever more daring and proficient in their exploits, they posed a very real threat to the might of Spain. The colonies and trade routes they established were soon the foundation on which England, in later years, built her empire.

W.S.Bulita

WORLD TOUR

Between 1577–80 Francis Drake completed his circumnavigation of the world, the first Englishman to do so. On his return, he became a national hero and was rewarded the following year by being knighted by Elizabeth aboard his ship, the *Golden Hind*.

PART-TIME NAVY

It was expensive to keep ships in constant service. When not required they were laid up in port and their crews paid off.

PRIDE OF THE FLEET

The '*Ark Royal*', shown here, was the flagship of the English navy. New designs by such shipwrights as Matthew Baker, made English ships much more manoeuvrable than those used by our enemies and played a key role in establishing England as a naval power.

RICHES FROM ABROAD

Elizabethan explorers brought back more than gold when they returned from distant parts of the globe. Merchants became extremely rich as the demand grew for new foodstuffs and materials from abroad.

'AT THE COURT OF QUEEN ELIZABETH....'

As Elizabeth's prestige and status grew throughout Europe, England came to be recognised as a growing world power. Many foreign ambassadors visited her at court to strike trade deals and negotiate political alliances to improve their country's position should England ever replace Spain as the dominant power in Europe. Here, she receives two Dutch officials in the Privy Chamber.

THE ARMADA ...

THE BUILD UP

*E*ver since Henry VIII's break with the Church of Rome, England had been under threat of invasion from the Catholic countries of Europe, especially after the Pope excommunicated Elizabeth in 1580. Spain was the most powerful country in Europe at that time and Philip II needed little persuasion to lead an invasion force against England, particularly as Elizabeth's navy openly inflicted acts of piracy on his fleet. In 1587 a council of war decided to launch a combined offensive against England. An armada of ships would be sent to the Netherlands, where they would collect a huge army and launch an offensive on the Kent coast, and afterwards march on London.

KEY

Catholic

Protestant

area of mixed faith

Othodox Christian and Islam

RELIGIOUS DIVISIONS

This map shows the political and religious divisions of Europe at the time of the Armada. By sending a force against England, Spain hoped to reunite Europe under Catholicism.

Lisbon
PORTU

A LOVE SCORNED

Philip II, King of Spain, was Elizabeth's brother-in-law. In 1554 he had married Mary, her Catholic half-sister, and had offered his hand in marriage to Elizabeth soon after her succession, but she refused him.

EARLY WARNING SYSTEM

A system of beacons around the coast warned of the Armada's approach. Each beacon, within sight of its neighbours, could convey a warning the length of the country in minutes.

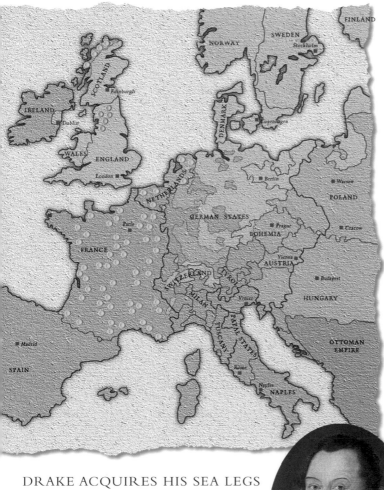

THE ROUTE OF THE ARMADA

The map above shows the route taken by the Armada. It set out from Lisbon on 20th May 1588 only to be scattered by bad weather. On 12th July, after revictualling and repairs, it set out again from La Coruna, in northern Spain, arriving in the Channel, off the Scilly Isles, on 19th July.

DRAKE ACQUIRES HIS SEA LEGS

Sir Francis Drake was born at Tavistock, Devon, in c.1541, though he learned his seafaring skills on the River Medway, in Kent, after his father, a naval chaplain, transferred to Chatham Dockyard around 1550.

...THE ARMADA

THE BATTLE COMMENCES

The Spanish Armada consisted of 138 ships in all, comprising 24 galleons, 40 merchantmen converted for war, 25 hulks to carry supplies and several other smaller vessels. By comparison, the English had 21 first-line ships and 40 of the second-line, with numerous support vessels, so the fleets were evenly matched. The English had an estimated 14,000 men compared with the Spanish total of about 24,000, but had 2000 cannons, nearly double the `Spanish number. The commander of the Spanish fleet was the Duke of Medina Sidonia. The English knew that the Spanish fleet was being amassed against them and tried to intersect it by launching a surprise attack before the Armada left Spanish waters. Unfortunately, bad weather foiled their plans and the English were driven back to port on the same day that the Spanish left La Coruna for the Channel.

THE BATTLE PLAN

This map shows how the course of the battle fared, from the first sighting of the Armada off the Lizard in Cornwall, to the final routing as a result of the havoc caused by the fireships off Calais.

THE ARMADA IS SIGHTED

According to unsubstantiated tradition, when Drake heard news at Plymouth that the Armada had been sighted, he insisted on finishing his game of bowls first.

RUNNING BATTLE

The English captains stole the advantage by performing several daring manoeuvres, but they were unable to strike at the heart of the Armada. A week-long running battle ensued as the prevailing wind carried the Armada towards its destination.

FRANKLYN'S CIGARETTES.

DRAKES GAME OF BOWLS

AN ILL WIND

Initially, it looked as if all would be lost when the prevailing wind and tide prevented most of the English fleet from leaving harbour. The skill of the English captains in managing to put to sea at all dismayed the Spanish.

FIRE IN THE NIGHT

The Armada successfully reached Calais and anchored, awaiting the arrival of their allies in Flanders. On the night of 28th July eight fireships, hulks laden with pitch and gunpowder, were set alight and cast adrift by the English amongst the Spanish fleet. The Spanish captains panicked and made for the open sea. Although the fireships did not actually set fire to any enemy ships, they succeeded in breaking their formation. This proved to be the turning point in the battle and the following day the scattered Armada was attacked mercilessly by the English. The Spanish fleet fled into the North Sea with the English in hot pursuit.

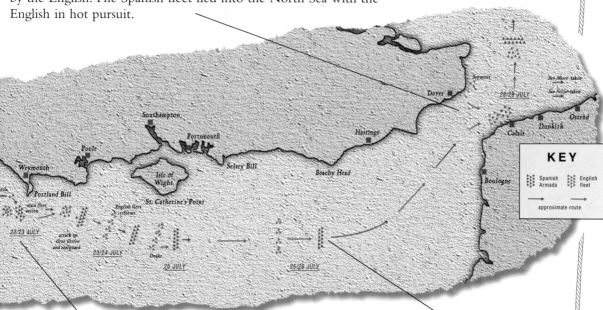

KEY

Spanish Armada

English fleet

→ approximate route

THE BATTLE RAGES

The Armada was formed into a crescent shaped formation and moved slowly up the Channel towards Calais. The first major engagement with the English fleet took place off Portland Bill, Dorset.

OUT-MANOEUVRED

Despite being out-manoeuvred by the English fleet, and suffering some losses, the Spanish maintained their tight formation and continued steadily up the Channel towards Calais.

...THE ARMADA

THE FLIGHT

Although the English had given a good account of themselves, the Armada succeeded in reaching its first objective, Calais, where they were to be joined by the Duke of Parma's army to invade England, but Dutch rebels prevented Parma's ships from putting to sea. Of the 138 ships that set out from Spain only 67 returned, most falling victim to the treacherous seas around Scotland and Ireland. The crews were ravaged by hunger and disease. Philip was devastated by the news that his grand plan had failed and, although in a few years his navy was stronger than ever, Spain never fully recovered from the humiliating defeat.

THE FLIGHT OF THE ARMADA

This map shows the route taken by the Armada in retreat. Prevailing winds aided their escape around the coasts of Scotland and Ireland. Howard pursued them for three days before returning home to victory celebrations.

COMMANDER OF THE FLEET

The queen's Catholic cousin, Lord Charles Howard of Effingham, was chosen to command the English fleet. Although not a professional sailor, he was a strong and able commander, which Elizabeth needed to keep her sometimes impetuous sea captains in check.

THE ARMADA JEWEL

This enamelled-gold jewel, set with diamonds and rubies, is said to have been given by Elizabeth to Sir Thomas Heneage, Vice-Chamberlain, after the defeat of the Armada.

HEARTS OF OAK

John Hawkins had the fighting vessels of the English navy rebuilt to bold new designs. Previously, ships were little more than floating fighting platforms, but the new ships were sleeker and equipped with many more guns, capable of firing broadside.

THE CHATHAM CHEST

Following the defeat of the Armada, Hawkins and Drake set up a voluntary fund for the support of distressed seamen, held at Chatham Dockyard in this chest.

DRAKE'S DRUM

When this drum was beaten aboard Drake's ship the men mustered for battle. After the defeat of the Armada, many legends sprang up around the drum, including one that says Drake will return from the grave to fight for England if ever it is beaten.

POLITICAL INTRIGUES

Somervites Paste to Kill the Quene

TIT-FOR-TAT

The Catholic John Somerville plotted to shoot Elizabeth in 1583, but his plan failed and he committed suicide in the Tower. A Bond of Association was afterwards formed whereby if Elizabeth's life was again threatened, the imprisoned Mary Queen of Scots would be executed, whether she was involved or not.

Throughout her reign, Elizabeth was surrounded by political intrigue as her various courtiers jostled for position and power. Towards the end of her reign, Robert Devereux, Earl of Essex, became her 'favourite' and was sent to Ireland to solve the crisis developing there. The Irish often formed an uneasy alliance with Spain, making England vulnerable to attack from that quarter. Several attempts were made to colonise Ireland with Protestant settlers, but they met with the same stout resistance experienced by colonists in America. Because Elizabeth relied so heavily on privateers to attain her position of power, the way was clear for them to amass huge personal fortunes, especially as new trade routes were opened up around the world. A more than generous tax system allowed the rich to keep much of their wealth, but at the expense of the royal purse. The situation was made worse by the mounting cost of the ongoing wars with Spain and Ireland.

OPEN REVOLT IN IRELAND

In 1598 the Earl of Tyrone inflicted a humiliating defeat on the English at the 'Battle of the Yellow Ford', near Armagh. This sparked off a general uprising amongst the Irish and many Protestant settlers were put to death. Elizabeth blamed the defeat partly on Essex's mishandling of the situation.

THE COLONIES
TAKE ROOT

While the opening of new
trade routes was Elizabeth's
primary concern, others
favoured colonisation to
establish a foothold in the
New World. Richard
Grenville, seen here
surrendering to the Spanish
in 1591, was foremost
amongst these, though most
of the early colonies failed.

EVENTS OF
ELIZABETH'S LIFE

~1577~
Drake sets out to
circumnavigate the world

~1580~
Drake returns from
his circumnavigation
of the world.
Elizabeth excommunicated
by the Pope

~1581~
Drake knighted.
Edmund Campion
executed

~1583~
John Somerville attempts
to assassinate Elizabeth

TRAITOR'S GATE

The old water gate, known as Traitor's
Gate, is where water-borne prisoners were
brought into the Tower of London to face
imprisonment or execution, including
Elizabeth herself when she
was imprisoned
for a short
while by
Mary I.

TRUSTED FRIENDS

The queen was constantly on
her guard from assassination
attempts, so she surrounded
herself with trusted friends
at all times, as shown in this
procession.

AN AGE OF DISCOVERY

The journeys of Elizabethan explorers are all the more incredible because many of the seas they crossed were uncharted. They had little way of knowing if they would return from their voyages or perish in the attempt. Captains, such as Drake, were also extremely skilled and capable navigators and map-makers. The continuing war with Spain closed many of England's traditional trading routes in Europe, so the need to open up new ones in other parts of the world became more pressing. Elizabeth herself sponsored many of the voyages and is reputed to have made 4,000% profit on her original investment from Drake's circumnavigation of the world.

AFTERMATH OF THE ARMADA

The good old days experienced by English privateers, of attacking Spanish outposts and vessels, almost at will, were gone following the defeat of the Armada. Spanish defences improved radically and Drake's last expedition to Porto Rico failed. He died of dysentery in 1596 and was buried at sea off Porto Bello, in the Caribbean.

SEARCH FOR THE STARS

As journeys became more adventurous, and so more perilous, the need for more sophisticated equipment became more pressing. Mathematicians and astronomers throughout Europe turned their attentions towards developing more accurate navigational instruments, aided by information brought back by the explorers. A Polish astronomer, Nicolaus Copernicus, first suggested that the Earth rotated on its axis and orbited around the sun, an idea supported by John Dee, the queen's own astrologer and astronomer. He was also one of the foremost mathematicians of his time and carried out much pioneering work in calculating longitude by utilising the magnetic properties of lodestone.

EXOTIC FRUITS

The pineapple, a native fruit of Central and South America, was one of the many new plants brought back by the explorers. It quickly became a favourite delicacy at table.

NO SMOKE WITHOUT FIRE

Sir Walter Raleigh made smoking fashionable, though it was often regarded with suspicion. Here, his servant douses him with water, thinking him to be on fire.

STAPLE DIET

Potatoes were introduced from Virginia about 1596. Unlike other new foods, regarded with some suspicion, potatoes soon became accepted as part of the normal diet.

MERRIE ENGLAND

*F*or most ordinary people the real benefit brought about by Elizabeth's strong reign was that of stability. The civil wars that had raged between Protestants and Catholics during Mary's turbulent reign were at an end and the country was restored to a period of relative calm and prosperity. Although little of the wealth generated by Elizabeth's merchant adventurers found its way down to peasant level, most people welcomed the sense of normality that had returned to their lives. Elizabeth had succeeded in uniting a divided country and

a sense of national pride was felt by most people. For a while life was good, and there was much to celebrate and be grateful for.

POET COURTIER

Sir Philip Sydney, soldier, scholar, writer and poet, came to represent the epitome of all that was chivalrous at Elizabeth's court. He was mortally wounded at the Battle of Zutphen and was given a hero's funeral at St. Paul's Cathedral, an unprecedented honour.

VIRTUOSO

Elizabeth was herself an accomplished musician and could play several instruments.
The virginals (an early type of harpsichord) shown here bear the Boleyn family coat-of-arms.

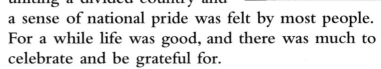

FAMILY ENTERTAINMENT

Professional musicians were employed to entertain guests in large households. Most people from wealthy families were expected to play an instrument or be able to sing.

EVENTS OF ELIZABETH'S LIFE

~1584~
Walter Raleigh establishes a colony in Virginia

~1585~
Drake sacks Santiago

COUNTRY DANCING

Most people in Elizabethan times needed little excuse to celebrate. Country dances were a popular form of ntertainment. The villagers here are dancing round a maypole as part of the May Day festivities.

TO BE OR NOT TO BE ...

Before Elizabeth's time most plays were performed by strolling players in the market place or inn yards. The first purpose-built theatres were erected in London in 1576. William Shakespeare was the most popular actor and dramatist of his day and often gave personal readings to the queen at court.

CHURCH MATTERS

The formation of the Church of England was something of a compromise, introduced by the opportunist Henry VIII, who merely took advantage of the growing tide of Protestantism sweeping across Europe to satisfy his personal ends. As long ago as the 14th century church reformers such as John Wycliffe had tried to introduce new ideas into Catholic doctrines. Catholics objected to any changes, while Protestant extremists felt the new Anglican Church did not go far enough, but it was generally welcomed when compared to the religious persecutions of Mary I's reign.

THE ROOT OF ALL EVIL

Elizabeth was a very devout Christian and felt that strong religious belief held the key to good government and everyone's general well-being:
'One matter toucheth me so nearly as I may not overskip - religion, the ground on which all other matters ought to take root, and being corrupted, may marr the whole tree.'

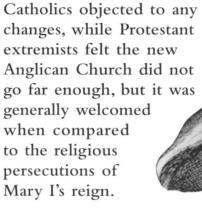

IN DEFIANCE OF ROME

Anti-Catholic feelings were rife throughout Europe in the 16th century. This woodcut shows the Pope as anti-Christ.

PERSECUTION

Witchcraft was still punishable by death and was not finally abolished as a crime until 1736.

THE WITCHES' SABBAT

Anyone who still practised the old pagan ways was generally termed a witch. However, many villages still tolerated a witch, or 'wise woman', in their midst, usually for their medical or fortune-telling abilities, even though witchcraft was illegal.

FIRST ARCHBISHOP

Matthew Parker was appointed Elizabeth's first Archbishop of Canterbury. He adopted a middle-of-the-road stance, rejecting the extreme religious views of both Catholic and Protestant, supporting the monarchy as head of the new Anglican Church.

FAMILY VALUES

Elizabethan families set great store by family values. The church instructed people to fear God and urged parents to teach the scriptures and encourage their children to say their prayers.

THE VIRGIN QUEEN

*A*t the beginning of her reign Elizabeth is recorded as saying that she already considered herself to be married, to 'the Kingdom of England' and referred to her coronation ring as a symbol of that union. She was often referred to as 'Gloriana', the pure and beautiful maiden. Throughout her long reign, however, the queen had many suitors, any one of whom might have become her husband and given her an heir, but later on her political advisers positively encouraged her to remain a spinster. She had proved herself to be a strong-willed ruler, much-loved by her people, and many feared that she might lose that popularity if she married and were influenced by a husband less able than herself.

APPEARANCES CAN BE DECEPTIVE

The queen tried to hide her age, and the scars left by smallpox, in later years with the overuse of cosmetics. Her face and neck were heavily powdered and painted white, giving her a very pallid appearance.

PERSONAL HYGIENE

Elizabeth was quite fastidious for her day and took great care over her personal hygiene. She carried a pomander, filled with fragrant herbs and perfumes, to combat the often unpleasant smells encountered in Tudor households.

BUSINESS AS USUAL

The Royal Exchange, in London, built by the financier Sir Thomas Gresham and opened by the queen in 1571, was an outward sign of the growing prosperity of England during Elizabeth's reign. Rich merchants from home and abroad gathered there to conduct their business.

STRICT STANDARDS

One of the many standards introduced by Elizabeth to control unscrupulous merchants was this set of bronze weights, used as the official standard for all commercial weights.

YOUNG AT HEART

In later years the queen was said to be almost bald and wore a wig of thick red hair to appear more youthful. She had also lost many of her teeth, which impaired her speech.

EVENTS OF ELIZABETH'S LIFE

~1596~
Potatoes first introduced from America.
Attack on Cadiz by Earl of Essex

~1598~
Battle of the Yellow Ford, Armagh, Ireland.
Philip II of Spain dies.
William Cecil dies

~1601~
Robert Devereux, Earl of Essex, executed.
Elizabeth delivers her 'Golden Speech'

~1603~
Elizabeth dies (last Tudor monarch).
James I crowned as first Stuart monarch.
Raleigh arrested for treason by James I

THE END OF AN ERA

*I*n her last speech to parliament, known as the 'Golden Speech', Elizabeth, aware that her glorious time was nearly over, summed up her own reign thus: 'Though God has raised me high, yet this I count the glory of my crown – that I have reigned with your loves …. And though you have had, and may have, many princes more mighty and wise, sitting in this state, yet you never had, or shall have, any that will be more careful and loving.'

She knew the good times were over and troubles lay ahead, but she retained a sense of humility to the last. She was the first English monarch to give her name to an age.

LIFE TAKES ITS TOLL

This painting shows Elizabeth on her deathbed. By the time she died the queen was a tired old woman. She certainly suffered from bouts of depression towards the end of her reign, as she became increasingly aware perhaps that her time of greatness was nearly over.

FALL FROM GRACE

Sir Walter Raleigh, one of Elizabeth's favourites, fell from favour under James I. Convicted on a trumped-up charge of treason in 1603, he was imprisoned in the Tower of London for 15 years before being executed in 1618.

THE QUEEN'S SUCCESSOR

When Elizabeth died, childless, in 1603, succession passed to James Stuart, the son of Mary Queen of Scots and her closest living relative.

THE GOOD OLD DAYS

This effigy of Elizabeth is from her tomb in Westminster Abbey and shows the queen as a frail old lady. Her glorious reign had brought untold wealth to England, but by 1603 serious problems loomed ahead. Many of her trusted advisers were dead, inflation soared and the mounting cost of the wars with Spain and Ireland had left the exchequer virtually bankrupt.

THE FINAL JOURNEY

Elizabeth died on 24th March 1603 at Richmond Palace, from where her body was conveyed by royal barge to Whitehall in preparation for her funeral. This picture shows part of the impressive funeral procession on 28th April, making its way to Westminster Abbey, where an estimated 1600 mourners waited to pay their last respects. Her coffin was surmounted by an impressive effigy of the queen in crown and full royal regalia.

A GLOSSARY OF INTERESTING TERMS

Bull - A metallic seal, usually lead, used to seal official letters, particularly those issued by the Pope.

Excommunication - Exclusion from Holy Communion in the church. A person so excluded would be denied God's protection and prohibited from entering Heaven when they died.

First Fruits - Ecclesiastical taxes that were originally paid to the Pope but, after the breach with Rome, formed part of the royal revenue until 1703.

Neck-verse - A verse read from the Bible by a person awaiting execution who might read it aloud to show repentance and so, hopefully, save their neck.

Privateer - Sea captains who have permission from the ruling monarch to attack the ships of another country at will and steal their cargoes.

Recusant - Anyone who refused to acknowledge the monarchy as head of the Church of England, or who refused to attend Protestant services following the Reformation.

Sheriff - The head crown official (reeve) enforcing law and order in the counties (or shires) outside London, hence 'shire-reeve'.

Wardrobe - A special department within the royal household responsible for purchasing dry goods, principally clothes, furniture and upholstery. The room where most of these items were kept came to be known as the wardrobe, as later did the cupboards in the room, the meaning of the term is still applied today.

ACKNOWLEDGEMENTS

We would like to thank: Graham Rich and Elizabeth Wiggans for their assistance and David Hobbs for his map of the world.
Copyright © 2003 *ticktock* Entertainment Ltd,
Unit 2, Orchard Business Centre, North Farm Road, Tunbridge Wells, Kent, TN2 3XF, U.K. First published in Great Britain 1998.
All rights reserved. No part of this publication may be reproduced, stored in a retrieval system, or transmitted in any form or by any means electronic, mechanical, photocopying, recording or otherwise, without prior written permission of the copyright owner.
Picture research by Image Select. Printed in Egypt.

Acknowledgements: Picture Credits t=top, b=bottom, c=centre, l=left, r=right, OFC=outside front cover, IFC=inside front cover, IBC= inside back cover, OBC= outside front cover.
Ashmolean Museum, Oxford; 8tl & OBC. The Bodleian Library, Oxford (MS Ashmole 1758, fol.83v); 10/11cb. Private Collection/Bridgeman Art Library, London; IFC/1. Houses of Parliament. Westminster, London/Bridgeman Art Library, London; 3cl. Guildhall Art Gallery, Corporation of London/Bridgeman Art Library, London; 7t. Private Collection/Bridgeman Art Library, London; 21b. Private Collection/Bridgeman Art Library, London; 26tl & OBC. Victoria & Albert Museum, London/Bridgeman Art Library, London; 27t. British Library, London/Bridgeman Art Library, London; 30b. By permission of The British Library (562*.f.28, p.4); 26bl. Reproduced by courtesy of His Grace the Lord Archbishop of Canterbury - Copyright reserved to the Courtauld Institute of Art and the Church Commissioners - Photograph Courtauld Institute of Art; 27c. English Heritage Photographic Library; 6/7. The Fotomas Index; 26/27c & OFC. Glasgow Museums: The Stirling Maxwell Collection, Pollock House - A Sanchez Coello *Philip II*; 14l. Crown Copyright. Historic Royal Palaces (Photograph 5.0301009/1); 20/21c. Hulton Getty; 3b. The Mansell Collection; 13t. Mary Evans Picture Library; 2tl,2c, 3tr, 4tl, 5tl, 6tl, 7b, 9c, 11tr, 12bl, 13br, 15tl, 16b & OBC, 17b, 19l, 20tl, 20bl, 21t, 22bl, 23tr, 23cr & OBC, 24/25c, 25tl, 25r, 27br, 29tl, 29br, 30tl, 30/31c & OFC. Museum of London; 28cb, 28/29b. National Maritime Museum, London; 2b, 15b, 16/17t, 18l & OFC, 18br, 22tl & OFC. Reproduced by permission of Viscount De L'Isle, from his private collection; 9t. By courtesy of the National Portrait Gallery, London; OFCc, 5b, 8bl, 8r, 31tl. Plymouth City Museums & Art Gallery collection; 19b. By courtesy of the Board of Trustees of the Victoria & Albert Museum; 19t & OBC, 24b. By Courtesy of the Dean and Chapter of Westminster; 4/5c, 9bl, 28tl, 31r.

Every effort has been made to trace the copyright holders and we apologise in advance for any unintentional omissions. We would be pleased to insert the appropriate acknowledgement in any subsequent edition of this publication.

A CIP Catalogue for this book is available from the British Library. ISBN 1 86007 401 4